Holiday Histories

Cinco de Mayo

Aurora Colón García

Heinemann Library
Chicago, Illinois

©2008 Heinemann-Raintree
a division of Pearson Education Limited
Chicago, Illinois

Editorial: Rebecca Rissman
Design: Kimberly R. Miracle and Tony Miracle
Picture Research: Kathy Creech and Tracy Cummins
Production: Duncan Gilbert

Originated by Chroma Graphics (Overseas) Pte. Ltd
Printed and bound in China by South China Printing Co. Ltd.
The paper used to print this book comes from sustainable resources.

ISBN-13: 978-1-4329-1040-2 (hc)
ISBN-10: 1-4329-1040-X (hc)
ISBN-13: 978-1-4329-1048-8 (pb)
ISBN-10: 1-4329-1048-5 (pb)

12 11 10 09 08
10 9 8 7 6 5 4 3 2 1

Library of Congress Cataloging-in-Publication Data
Colón García, Aurora.
  Cinco de Mayo / Aurora Colón García.
    p. cm. -- (Holiday histories)
Summary: Discusses the holiday Cinco de Mayo, celebrated by Mexicans and Mexican Americans in remembrance of the Mexican army's defeat of the French army in Pubela, Mexico, in 1862.
Includes bibliographical references and index.
1st Edition ISBN 1-4034-3501-4 (HC), 1-4034-3686-X (Pbk.) 1. Cinco de Mayo (Mexican holiday)--History--Juvenile literature. 2. Mexico--Social life and customs--Juvenile literature. 3. Mexican Americans--Social life and customs--Juvenile literature. 4. Cinco de Mayo, Battle of, 1862--Juvenile literature. [1. Cinco de Mayo (Mexican holiday) 2. Mexico--Social life and customs. 3. Holidays.] I. Title. II. Series.
  F1233.C6523 2003
  394.262--dc21
                          2003007825

Acknowledgments
The author and publishers are grateful to the following for permission to reproduce photographs: ©Center Daily Times **p. 28-29**; ©Corbis **p. 5** (Paul Barton); ©Digitalrailroad **p.6** (UPI); ©The Granger Collection **pp. 9** (right), **10, 11, 12, 13, 14, 16** (all), **20, 21, 22**; ©John Andress **p. 23**; ©Magnum Photo **p. 7** (Eugene Richards); ©Mississippi Department of Archives and History **p. 24** (left); ©Photo Edit **p. 24** (Gary Conner); ©Photo Researchers, Inc. **p. 9** (left); ©SuperStock **pp. 8, 10, 15, 19, 26**; ©Theater Pix **p. 27** (Michael Brosilow).

Cover photograph reproduced with permission of ©Getty Images/Lonely Planet/Jerry Alexander

Contents

Some words are shown in bold, **like this**. You can find out what they mean by looking in the glossary.

A Day for Celebrating

¡Viva Cinco de Mayo! On May 5 floats are decorated. Dancers, singers, and children dressed in festive clothing ride on floats in parades.

Many Mexican-Americans celebrate their **heritage** on this day. They celebrate with parades, **festivals**, music, and dancing. They celebrate pride and freedom.

Celebrations from City to City

Cinco de Mayo is celebrated all across the country. The holiday is celebrated in Chicago, Denver, San Antonio, and many other cities.

This Cinco de Mayo celebration is in St. Louis.

In San Antonio, Texas, many people may clap to the beat of the popular Latino groups performing on stage in Market Square.

Celebrations in Mexico

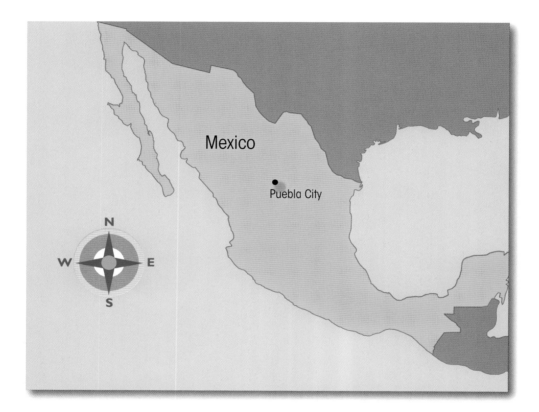

In the country of Mexico, many Mexicans celebrate Cinco de Mayo in a city called Puebla. Cinco de Mayo is also celebrated in many other cities in Mexico.

In Mexico, there are **festivals** and parades. At the festivals food is sold from booths decorated in bright colors. But why do we celebrate Cinco de Mayo?

Why Do We Celebrate?

Cinco de Mayo means May 5 in Spanish.
On May 5, 1862, a **battle** took place in Puebla,
Mexico. This holiday celebrates the Mexican army
winning the battle against the French army.

Cinco de Mayo celebrates the **unity** and **pride** of the Mexican people. Today at the **festivals** men dress up as soldiers and pretend to have a fight. Mexico always wins in these make-believe battles.

Mexican Independence

During the 1800s, Mexico was under the control of Spain. On September 15, 1810, Father Miguel Hidalgo united the Mexican people. He encouraged the Mexicans to fight for their **freedom**.

Mexico was freed from Spain in 1821. The Mexicans did not know how to run the country. They had two different groups of people trying to run the country. This caused many problems. The Mexican government was not united.

Mexican-American War

After Mexico was free from Spain, Mexicans began to argue with people from the United States. The United States government wanted Mexico's land. Mexico would not give up its land. Mexico and the United States went to war.

This war was the Mexican-American War. The United States won the war. Mexico had to give up half of its land to the United States.

Money Trouble

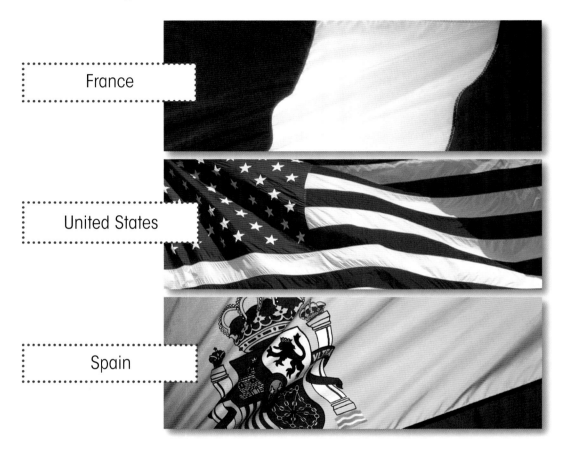

France

United States

Spain

After the Mexican-American War, Mexico had very little money in its **treasury**. Mexico had used a lot of money to fight in many **battles**. Mexico owed money to France, Spain, and the United States.

Benito Juárez was the president. He told the other countries he would pay them later. He used the little money Mexico had to help the Mexican people.

France

Napoleon III was the ruler of France.
He was very angry when Mexico did not pay.
He decided to take land from Mexico.

The French wanted to rule Mexico. They wanted to
add Mexico's land to their government. Napoleon III
sent his army to Mexico to try to take over.

The French Army

The French army was very strong. The men in the French army were well trained. They knew how to fight in **battle** and had good weapons.

In 1861, the French army attacked Veracruz, Mexico and won the battle. The French took over Veracruz. They began to move toward Puebla.

The Mexican Army

The men in the Mexican army were not well trained. Their weapons were old. The Mexican army was small. They did not know how to fight in **battles**.

This statue of General Ignacion Zaragoza stands in Puebla, Mexico.

President Benito Juárez sent General Ignacion Zaragoza and his soldiers to Puebla to stop the French soldiers. He led the brave men in the Mexican army into battle.

The Battle of Puebla

General Zaragoza put his men on the two hills outside the city of Puebla. The French soldiers went up the hills to attack the Mexican solidiers. The brave Mexican soldiers fired their **muskets** and cannons at them.

The French soldiers went back down the hill. During the **battle** it began to rain. The rain made it hard for the French soldiers to come back up the hills. The sides of the hills turned into mud. The French **retreated**.

Victory for the Mexicans

The Mexican soldiers fought hard. They won the battle against the powerful French army. The battle was called the La Batalla de Puebla. The Mexican people finally had a **common cause**.

Mexicans were proud to say, "¡Yo soy Mexicano!"
It was a victory against great odds!

An American Celebration

Later, many Mexicans began to move to the United States to find jobs. When they came to the United States they brought along their **customs** and celebrations.

Their celebrations have become part of the American culture.

Important Dates

Cinco de Mayo

1810	Father Miguel Hidalgo unites the Mexicans
1821	Mexico gains independence from Spain
1846	Mexican-American War
1861	Veracruz surrenders to the French
1862	Mexico wins the Battle of Puebla
1960s	Mexican-American students at California State University, Los Angeles, hold the first Cinco de Mayo celebration
1995	Greater East Austin Youth League begins the annual Austin Cinco de Mayo music festival

Glossary

battle fight between armies

common cause supported movement

custom usual way of doing something

festival celebration

heritage birthright

muskets large, heavy gun

pride having self-respect

retreated withdraw

treasury where the government keeps its money

untrained not prepared or instructed

unity stand together

Find Out More

Flanagan, Alice K. *Cinco de Mayo.* Minneapolis: Compass Point, 2003.

Gnojewski, Carol. *Cinco de Mayo Crafts.* Berkeley Heights, NJ: Enslow Publishers, Inc., 2005.

MacMillan, Dianne M. *Mexican Independence Day and Cinco de Mayo.* Berkeley Heights, NJ: Enslow Publishers, Inc., 2008.

Index